What Do You Feed Your Donkey On?

RHYMES FROM A BELFAST CHILDHOOD

Collected by COLETTE O'HARE / Illustrated by JENNY RODWELL

COLLINS

For Isa Quinlan

Collins
London · Glasgow · New York · Cleveland
Sydney · Auckland · Johannesburg · Toronto

First published 1978
© This collection Colette O'Hare 1978
© Illustrations Jenny Rodwell 1978
ISBN 0 00 183703 6

Library of Congress Cataloging in Publication Data

Colette O'Hare/Jenny Rodwell

What do you feed your donkey on?

SUMMARY: An illustrated collection of traditional rhymes, songs, and street chants from Belfast.
1. Nursery rhymes, Irish. 2. Belfast—Cries. 3. Street music and musicians. [1. Nursery rhymes, Irish. 2. Belfast—Cries. 3. Cries. 4. Street music and musicians.] I. O'Hare, Colette. II. Rodwell, Jenny.
PZ8.3.W56   398.8   77-17155
ISBN 0-00-183703-6
ISBN 0-00-183734-6 lib. bdg.

Made and printed in Great Britain by
W. S. Cowell Ltd Ipswich

Introduction

"What do you feed your donkey on?" was a question often teasingly posed by children to a trader as he drove his cart around the Belfast streets of many years ago. The reply of "Any auld rags!", "Herrings alive!", or "Any refuse, refuse, refuse!" never failed to amuse and delight. Although the horse-drawn cart has all but disappeared, the tradition of children's street games is everywhere alive and vital, and most of the limericks, ballads, chants, and songs in this collection can still be heard today.

All of these rhymes have been carefully and accurately set down as they have traditionally been recited or sung in Ireland. Some of them have their counterparts in the folk literature of other cultures as well, and will be recognized by the reader as variations of familiar verses, skipping-rope songs, and chants.

Charlie Walker sells fish,
Three ha'pence a dish,
Cut the heads off,
Cut the tails off,
Charlie Walker sells fish.

Bangor boat's away,
We have no time to stay,
One in a boat, two in a boat,
Bangor boat's away.

My Aunt Jane, she called me in,
Gave me tea out of her wee tin,
Half a bap, sugar on the top,
Three black lumps out of her wee shop.

Datsie-dotsie, miss the rope, you're outie-o,
If you'd've been, where I'd have been,
You wouldn't have been put outie-o,
All the money's scarce, people out of workie-o,
Datsie-dotsie, miss the rope, you're outie-o.

Vote, vote, vote, for Anne Marie Aicken,
In comes Paddy at the door, aye-o,
For Paddy is the one who will have a bit of fun,
And we'll never vote for Anne Marie anymore, aye-o.

Charlie Chaplin went to France,
To teach all the cannibals how to dance,
With a heel, toe, a burlie-o,
Miss the rope, and out you go.

At the auld Lammas Fair boy,
Were you ever there,
At the auld Lammas Fair in Ballycastle-o.
Did you treat your Mary Ann,
To some dulse and yellowman,
At the auld Lammas Fair in Ballycastle-o.

Barney Hughes's bread,
Sticks to your belly like lead,
Not a bit of wonder,
You rift like thunder,
Barney Hughes's bread.

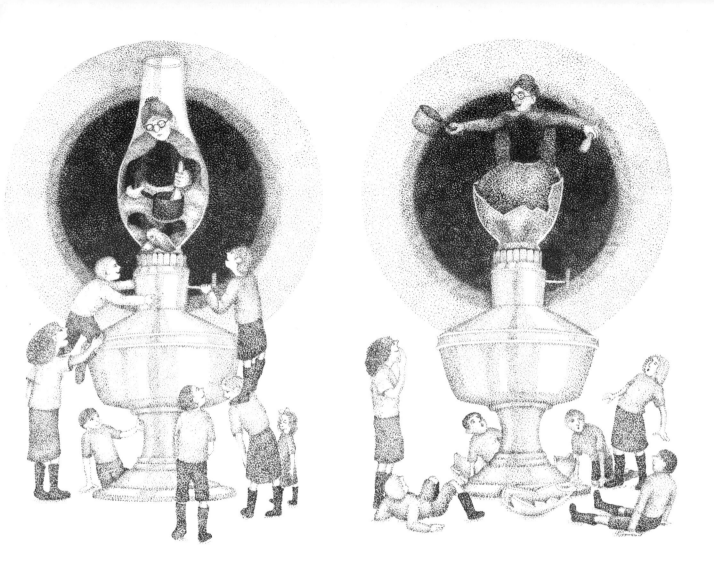

There was an old woman who lived in a lamp,
She had no room to beetle her champ,
So she up with the beetle and broke the lamp,
Now she's got room to beetle her champ.

On the Oldpark Road, where I did dwell,
Lived a butcher's son, whom I knew so well,
He courted me, till my heart was sore,
Then left me standing at the door.

He took a strange girl on his knee,
And he told her things that he never told me,
And now I know the reason why,
Because she had more gold than I.

But her gold will melt,
And his love will die,
And she will be as poor as I.

Wall flowers, wall flowers, growing up so high,
All pretty children do not like to cry,
Except Keady O'Hare, she's the only one,
So fright! For shame! So fright! For shame!
And turn her back to the wall again.

Skinny-me-link melodian legs,
Big banana feet,
Went to the pictures,
And couldn't get a seat,
When he got a seat,
He fell fast asleep,
Skinny-me-link melodian legs,
Big banana feet.

Over the garden wall,
I let the baby fall,
Me Ma came out,
And give me a clout,
Over the garden wall.

Over the garden wall,
I let the baby fall,
Me Ma came out
And give me a clout,
She give me another,
To match the other,
Over the garden wall.

Granny, Granny Grey,
Will you let me out to play,
I won't go near the water,
Or chase the ducks away.

Holy Mary, Mother of God,
Pray for me and Tommy Todd,
I'm a Fenian and he's a Prod,
Holy Mary, Mother of God.

I sent McCann
For a can of stout,
McCann came running in,
And said me can was running out.

Our Queen can bowl her leg, bowl her leg, bowl her leg,
Our Queen can bowl her leg,
BOWL HER LEG.
Our Queen can ate a hard bap, ate a hard bap, ate a hard bap,
Our Queen can ate a hard bap,
ATE A HARD BAP.

Granny in the kitchen,
Doing a bit of stitching,
In comes a bogie man,
And chases Granny out.
Ah, says Granny, that's not fair,
Ah, says the bogie man, I don't care.

Our auld dog,
He doesn't mind,
He'll knock off your dinner,
Then bite your behind.

Ah Ma, give us a penny,
To see the big giraffe,
He's got a pimple on his —
Ah Ma, give us a penny,
To see the big giraffe.

Eggs and Bacon.
I like eggs and bacon.
If you think I'm going to sing about it,
You're mistaken.

Will you come to my wee party,
Will you come?
Bring your own cup and saucer,
And a bun.

Ah Ma, will you buy me a, buy me a, buy me a,
Ah Ma, will you buy me a,
Buy me a banana.

Ah Ma, will you take a bite, take a bite, take a bite,
Ah Ma, will you take a bite,
A bite of my banana.

Ah Ma, you took it all, took it all, took it all,
Ah Ma, you took it all,
Took all my banana.

Notes

This song refers to the May Queen tradition, when competition between different districts or streets might call for a trial of strength between rival Queens, above and beyond a mere question of finery. To "bowl" the leg is a Charleston-type movement.

Not everyone relishes the idea of being asked to do a turn at a birthday party, family gathering or sing-song. This "recitation" could always be relied on to get a laugh – as well as allow the reluctant performer to beat a hasty retreat. *Charlie McGrory* (following page) was used in a similar way.

I'll tell you a story,
Of Charlie McGrory,
A hole in the wall,
And that's it all.